Amazing Cars

WRITTEN BY
TREVOR LORD

PHOTOGRAPHED BY
DAVE KING

DORLING KINDERSLEY
London · New York · Stuttgart

A Dorling Kindersley Book

Project editor Louise Pritchard
Art editor Mark Regardsoe
Senior art editor Julia Harris
Senior editor Helen Parker
Production Shelagh Gibson

Illustrations by Bruce Hogarth and Julie Anderson
Cars supplied by National Motor Museum at Beaulieu, John Lewis (pp 14-15),
Keith Atkinson (pp 16-17), International Automotive Design (pp 24-25)
Special thanks to Carl Gombrich for research; Mike Dunning for photography (pp 24-25);
Andy Saunders for his "Amazing minis" (p 17)

Chitty Chitty Bang Bang by permission of Warfield Productions Inc.;
James Bond Aston Martin DB5 by permission of Eon Productions Ltd.

First published in Great Britain in 1992 by
Dorling Kindersley Limited
9 Henrietta Street, London WC2E 8PS

A CIP catalogue record for this book is available from the British Library

ISBN 0-86318-730-7

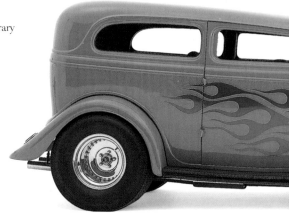

Colour reproduction by Colourscan, Singapore
Printed in Italy by A. Mondadori Editore, Verona

Contents

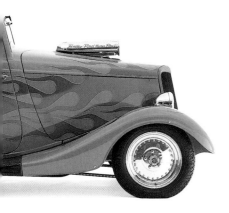

What is a car?

In the last 100 years, few things have changed our lives and the look of our surroundings more than the car. It is a truly amazing invention.

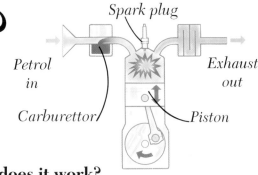

Spark plug

Petrol in

Carburettor

Exhaust out

Piston

How does it work?

Most cars are powered by a petrol engine. Petrol is mixed with air in the carburettor. A spark from a spark plug makes this mixture explode. This pushes a piston down, which turns the car's wheels.

Hood rolled back

On wheels

A car would be useless without wheels. It is moved and steered by the wheels and stopped by the brakes, which are connected to the wheels. And the tyres are filled with air to make the ride comfortable.

Boot for luggage

Farm vehicle

The Citroën 2CV was designed in the 1930s to use in rural areas. The designers were asked to make a car which would carry two people, 50 kg of produce or a small barrel, and drive over a field with a box of eggs without breaking any.

H359 FJ

Slow moving

There are millions of cars in the world today, so roads get overcrowded. The average speed of traffic in some cities is the same now as it was before we had cars!

Altered to fit

Cars can be altered for people with disabilities. For example, the brakes can be controlled by hand instead of by foot.

How many are there?

Cars are useful but they cause problems. The people on the Channel Island of Sark do not have cars – only bicycles and horse-drawn carts.

Bonnet

Is this a car?

A car is a motorized vehicle that carries passengers on the road. Most cars are easy to recognize, but some don't look like cars at all.

Happy families

A car can be one of the family. It goes shopping and may go on holiday. Some people even give their cars a name!

A 2CV is just over 3.8 m long. Its top speed is 70 miles per hour (mph) (112 kilometres per hour [km/h])

Birth of the car

The first cars did not look like cars at all. Many of the ideas were copied from other kinds of transport.

Horseless carriages

Some early cars were simply horse-drawn carriages fitted with an engine. These cars were difficult to steer without the help of the horses.

Making claims

In 1895, the Pennington Company said that their car could carry nine people, drive at 40 mph (64 km/h) and had tyres which were puncture-proof. This of course was not true.

Uphill struggle

Early cars had the petrol tank fitted high up to let the petrol flow down to the engine. But if cars were driven up a very steep hill, the petrol would flow away from the engine. The solution was to drive up backwards!

Right or wrong

Small boats are steered using a tiller. Some of the first cars were also steered using a tiller. To turn the car to the right, the tiller was moved to the left. To turn the car to the left, the tiller was moved to the right – confusing!

Tiller

This Peugeot is only 2.6 m long

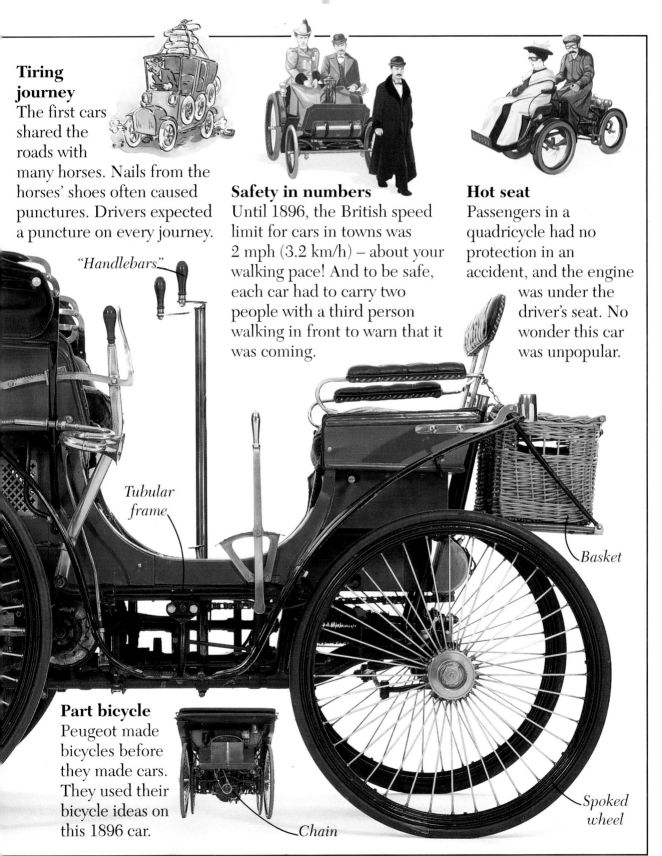

Tiring journey
The first cars shared the roads with many horses. Nails from the horses' shoes often caused punctures. Drivers expected a puncture on every journey.

"Handlebars"

Safety in numbers
Until 1896, the British speed limit for cars in towns was 2 mph (3.2 km/h) – about your walking pace! And to be safe, each car had to carry two people with a third person walking in front to warn that it was coming.

Hot seat
Passengers in a quadricycle had no protection in an accident, and the engine was under the driver's seat. No wonder this car was unpopular.

Tubular frame

Basket

Part bicycle
Peugeot made bicycles before they made cars. They used their bicycle ideas on this 1896 car.

Chain

Spoked wheel

On the road

Sports cars are the fastest cars on the road and are built to be fun to drive. No one worries about the comfort of the passengers – if there are any!

Gliding along

The Mercedes Gullwing is very low. To make it easier to get in and out, the doors open upwards making the car look like a flying gull.

To begin with

One of the first sports cars was the Vauxhall Prince Henry with a top speed of 75 mph (120 km/h). This is slow for today but it was fast for 1915 when the car was made.

Happy birthday

In 1987, the Italian Ferrari company was 40 years old. To celebrate, they built a new, very special and very fast supercar called the F40. Only a few were made.

Beetle in disguise

This Porsche 911 was designed by the grandson of Ferdinand Porsche, the designer of the Volkswagen Beetle, and some bits look just the same. The Porsche goes much faster than a Beetle though!

This Porsche is about 4.3 m long from nose to tail

Looks good

One of the top sports cars in the 1950s was the American Chevrolet Corvette. It had stunning good looks and could accelerate even faster than a Jaguar.

A car to match

In the 1960s it was important to be fashionable. And the most fashionable car was the E-Type Jaguar. It had a top speed of 150 mph (240 km/h).

D.I.Y. motoring

Lotus built only about 3,000 of their Lotus 7 sports cars and most of them were sold as kits. The customer bought the parts and, luckily, a set of instructions.

That's fast!

The top speed of the Lamborghini Diablo is over 200 mph (320 km/h). It is claimed to be the fastest road car in the world. The huge engine can rocket the car from a standstill to 60 mph (96 km/h) in four seconds!

"Whale tail" to push the car down on to the road for better grip

Working cars

Many cars are specially built to do a job and they go to work every day. Others are everyday cars altered to work on special jobs.

Just like a frog

An amphibian is an animal that lives on land and in water, such as a frog. We call cars that can travel on land and in water amphibious too. Amphibious cars can be very useful for getting up close to wildlife.

Making tracks

The first car to cross the Sahara Desert in Africa had tracks at the rear instead of wheels. The tracks gave better grip and prevented the car from sinking into the soft sand.

Called up

Cars were first used as ambulances during the First World War (1914-1918). They were altered to carry the wounded to hospital. Many nurses learnt to drive as part of their training.

Symbol to show taxi takes a wheel-chair

"For hire" light

London taxi

This car is specially designed and built to be a taxi. It has room for luggage in the front, next to the driver, and extra seats that flip down so the taxi can carry five people.

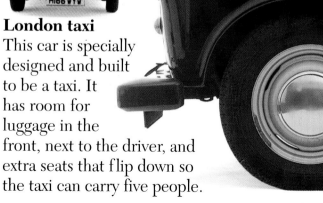

Fast worker

Police often drive at high speed. Their cars have flashing lights so we can see them coming – and a loud siren so we can hear them too!

Moving pictures

At sports events, TV companies often put a camera on a car so the camera person can keep up with the action. Citroëns are popular for this because they stay level and steady.

To the rescue

Some organizations help motorists whose cars have broken down. A mechanic comes in a car fitted with most of the tools and spare parts normally seen in a garage.

Aerial for computer radio which works out which taxi to call

Flip-down seat

This London taxi is 4.5 m long from bumper to bumper

Crazy cars

Cars are not always exactly as their owners want them. So they are customized – chopped up, added to, given new parts, and painted bright colours – until they look completely different.

Swanning along
This swan car was made in 1912. Its beak opens and shuts, its nostrils are exhaust pipes, and its eyes are electric lights.

War hero
"Jeepneys" were first built in the Philippines from American jeeps left behind after the Second World War. Today they are made using parts from more modern cars.

The roof has been lowered by 10 cm

Just my imagination
You can do almost anything you like to a car. With time and imagination, you can turn an ordinary car into a work of art.

The wheel arches have been enlarged to make room for these new wide wheels

Ahoy there!
This car used to be a speed-boat. Now, with three wheels, it is only for travelling on the road.

Amazing minis
These two Minis are even more mini than usual! They are perfect for squeezing in and out of small spaces, making parking much less of a problem.

Scoop for taking in air to cool the engine

Orange squash
Under the skin, this orange car is just a Mini. There is very little room inside, so the passengers are often squashed.

One in a thousand
In 1934, this Ford Sedan was like thousands of others. Now, it is lower, has a 7.5-litre Chevrolet engine, and has a top speed of 140 mph (224 km/h).

This customized Ford is now almost 5 m long

Travelling in style

Some cars are built for speed, some are made to be cheap to run. Other cars are designed to provide luxury, no matter what the cost.

Power guzzler

A "super-luxury" eight-seater Mercedes-Benz was introduced in the 1960s. Its many power-assisted features used up one sixth of the engine's power.

Cadillac comfort

This 1957 Cadillac is still thought to be luxurious today. Among its features are separate heating in the front and back, and seats which move electrically and store favourite positions in a memory.

Quality car

Duesenberg cars were made in the USA to rival the British Rolls-Royces. They were claimed to be "the world's finest automobiles". Only about 36 Duesenberg SJs were built.

This 1935 Duesenberg SJ is about 5 m long

Don't spill it

Rolls-Royces are famous for giving a quiet, smooth ride. In the 1930s, pupils at the Rolls-Royce school for chauffeurs had to drive a Phantom II with a glass of water balanced on the radiator – without spilling it!

Top class

The inside of this 1906 Renault was copied from a first-class railway carriage. The owner had wanted a tall car in which he would be able to wear his top hat.

Golf-club locker

Anyone for golf?

This 1935 Auburn was popular with Hollywood film stars. It was one of the first cars to have a radio. There was no room for luggage, but there was a special locker for golf-clubs instead.

Fit for a king

Leopold II was king of Belgium from 1865 to 1909. He was a large man so he had a car specially made with a wide seat shaped like his favourite armchair. His design became popular and was known as Roi des Belges style.

Duesenberg mascot known as a Duesenbird

Outside exhaust pipes

On the track

 Ever since cars first appeared, people have wanted to see who could drive the fastest. Racing in cars is now a popular sport. It is exciting, but it can also be dangerous.

In the right gear

Racing drivers today wear a crash helmet and a special suit to protect them in an accident. The first racing drivers just wore a cap – back to front to stop it blowing off!

Racing round the clock

One of the world's most famous car races is the Le Mans 24 Hours, in France. Every year, teams of drivers race the cars all through the day and night.

What a drag

Dragsters are the most powerful of all racing cars and can reach a speed of over 250 mph (400 km/h) in five seconds. A drag race takes place between two cars along a straight-line course which is only 1/4 mile (just over 400 m) long.

Smooth tyres used in dry weather

It's the pits

If a racing car needs to have new tyres during a race, the driver goes into the pits where mechanics can change the wheels in less than 10 seconds. Sometimes they refuel the car or change worn-out parts.

Air scoop to cool the brakes

Sucking the road

The fan on the back of this racing car pulls the air out from under the car. This sucks the car down on to the race track and helps it go around the corners faster.

Leading the way

When motor racing began, ordinary cars were raced along ordinary roads. They were often led through the smaller towns by a cyclist to stop them breaking the speed limit. A mechanic travelled in each car in case of a breakdown.

Racing on wings

The "wings" on this Formula One racing car work just like an aeroplane's but upside down. They hold the car down instead of lifting it up.

This Formula One car is 4.4 m long and 2.2 m wide

"Wing"

Famous cars

Cars, like people, can become famous for many reasons. How many of these famous cars do you recognize?

Tasty rolls

For some people, even a Rolls-Royce is not good enough. Pop star John Lennon made his Rolls-Royce easy to recognize with special paintwork.

Popemobile

The popemobile is a converted Range Rover used by Pope John Paul II. It is designed to give the crowd a good view of the pope as he travels round. The car has special puncture-proof tyres, and there are handles and a step at the back for the pope's bodyguards.

Speeding – Me?

When the first motorways were opened in Britain, they did not have a speed limit. Early one morning in 1964, an AC Cobra racing car was tested on the M1 at over 180 mph (288 km/h). A motorway speed limit of 70 mph (112 km/h) was introduced soon after!

Chitty Chitty Bang Bang is just over 7 m long, including the basket

Wing for flying

Over the moon

In 1971 the Apollo 15 spacecraft took the first car to the moon. This electric vehicle cost about £25 million ($60 million) to build and took 10 years to design.

Full of tricks

The film version of James Bond's Aston Martin DB5 had lots of special gadgets. It could produce an oil slick to trouble chasing cars, it had a bullet-proof shield at the back, and had an ejector seat to remove unwanted passengers!

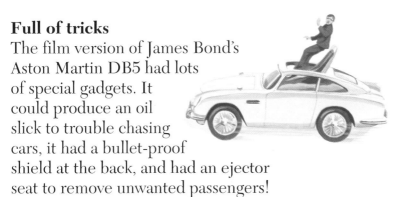

No-rust guarantee

DeLorean cars were made famous by the *Back to the Future* films, in which a car was a time machine. In real life DeLoreans are special too. They are not painted but they never rust because they are made of stainless steel.

Goes with a bang

The *Chitty Chitty Bang Bang* film car was based on real cars which raced in Britain in the 1920s. They were given their name because their noisy engine went chitty-chitty-bang-bang!

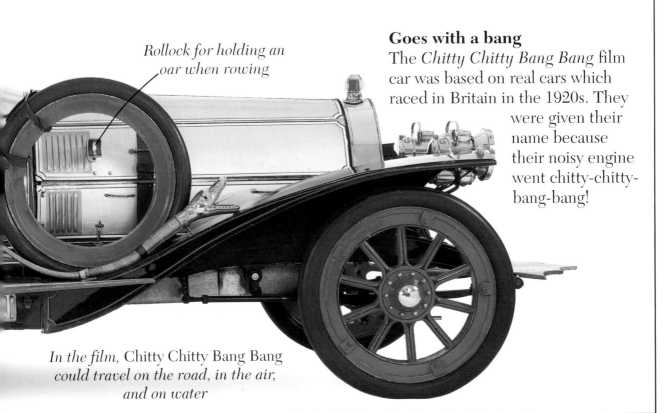

Rollock for holding an oar when rowing

In the film, Chitty Chitty Bang Bang *could travel on the road, in the air, and on water*

Into the future

Exciting new cars are being developed all the time. Most will not be built to go faster than cars can today, but will be designed to make driving safer and easier.

A bright idea

Sunraycer runs on solar energy. It has special panels which change sunlight into electrical energy. Unfortunately, solar-powered cars only work well in countries which have a lot of sunshine!

Keep your distance

In the future, drivers may be forced to drive safely because of sensors fitted in the car and under the road. The sensors will detect when a car is too close to the one in front and will stop it getting any closer.

Quieter towns

Battery-powered cars cause less pollution than petrol-engined cars. They are being developed to travel long distances without having to have their batteries recharged.

No more maps

One day, drivers will not need maps. They will tell a computer in the car where they want to go, and the computer will work out the best route. It will find out how to avoid traffic jams and bad weather too.

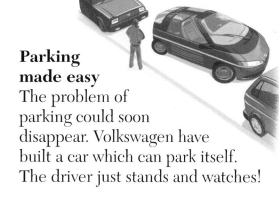

Parking made easy

The problem of parking could soon disappear. Volkswagen have built a car which can park itself. The driver just stands and watches!

Venus is about 4 m long

Home, James

Over 90% of road accidents are the fault of the driver. One day computers may do the driving.

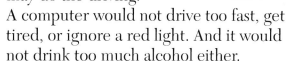

A computer would not drive too fast, get tired, or ignore a red light. And it would not drink too much alcohol either.

A view of the future

Venus is an experimental car – the only one of its kind to be built. It has two cameras to help the driver see the road in bad conditions. The cameras film in front and behind and show the views on a screen in the car.

Wheel inside "tyre-hugging pod" to stop road spray

Making a car

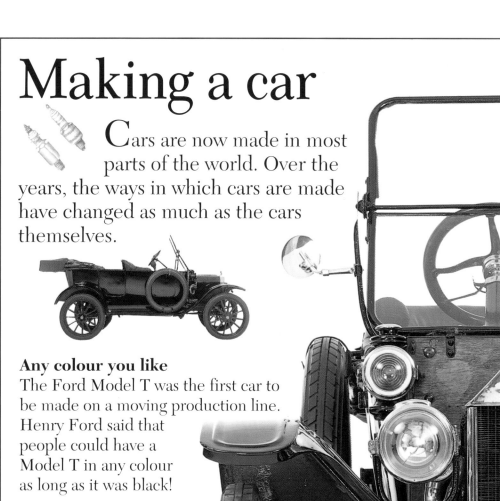

Cars are now made in most parts of the world. Over the years, the ways in which cars are made have changed as much as the cars themselves.

Any colour you like
The Ford Model T was the first car to be made on a moving production line. Henry Ford said that people could have a Model T in any colour as long as it was black!

Cars from rock
Today, car factories are as big as towns. Until recently at Ford's factory in Dagenham, England, the rock iron ore (from which steel is made) came by ship to one end of the factory and cars came out the other.

This 1914 Model T is 3.8 m long and 1.6 m wide

BE 278

Five years old
It can take five years for a new car to appear in the showroom. A design is drawn first, often with the help of a computer which can make changes easily.

Model car
A clay model of the car is built to test the shape for things such as how well the car will cut through the air. Changes are then made to the design if necessary.

Road test
Full-size working models are tested to see that the car works well and is safe, and even to see what would happen in a crash. Then real production begins.

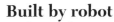

Built by robot
Today, robots are often used to make the body of cars. They can fit wheels and paint the bodies, but they do not drive the cars – yet!

Body work
When cars first became popular, makers of horse-drawn carriages began making car bodies instead.

What a difference
Aston Martin build 200 cars a year but Toyota make 5 million. So while Aston Martin are making one car, Toyota are making 25,000!

Record breakers

Since the beginning of motoring, some cars have stood out from all the others and now have a place in history. They are the record breakers.

Tail fin kept the car going straight

Aeroplane on wheels

In 1964 Donald Campbell drove *Bluebird* for a new land speed record (403.1 mph [648.72 km/h]). It is easy to imagine this car with wings. Who knows? Perhaps it would have flown.

We love the Beetles

The Volkswagen Beetle was first made in 1938. Over 20 million have been made, making it the most popular car of all time. Many people said it would never sell as it was too ugly!

The lengths people go to

One of the largest cars ever built was made in the USA. It has 26 wheels and is over 30 m long. It has a swimming pool and a helicopter landing pad. When it has to turn a corner it just bends in the middle.

A long way to go

A Honda car, *Genius E,* broke the record for the lowest petrol consumption – 6,409 miles per gallon (2,279 km per litre). If all cars did this, drivers would only buy petrol once every five years!

Fastest on land

In 1983 Richard Noble broke the land speed record. His jet-engined *Thrust 2* sped across 1 mile (1.6 km) of desert in California, USA – twice – at a speed of over 633 mph (1,013 km/h).

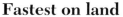

On your bike

The first land speed record was officially set in 1898 at 39 mph (63 km/h) – slower than the cycling record at the time!

Give me a lift

At 1.34 m long, the Peel is one of the smallest cars ever made. It has no reverse gear. The driver just gets out, grabs the handle at the back, and lifts the car round.

Driver's cockpit

Bluebird *is over 9 m long*